EUROPE

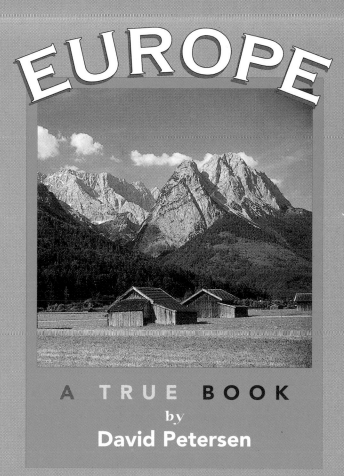

A TRUE BOOK

by

David Petersen

Children's Press®

A Division of Grolier Publishing

New York London Hong Kong Sydney
Danbury, Connecticut

Barcelona, Spain

Reading Consultant
Linda Cornwell
Learning Resource Consultant
Indiana Department of
Education

Visit Children's Press on the Internet at:
http://publishing.grolier.com

Library of Congress Cataloging-in-Publication Data

Petersen, David, 1946–
    Europe / by David Petersen.
        p.   cm. — (A True book)
    Includes bibliographical references and index.
    Summary: A brief overview of the geography, wildlife, history, and
people of Europe.
    ISBN 0–516–20766–0 (lib. bdg.)   0-516-26375-7 (pbk.)
    1. Europe—Juvenile literature. [1. Europe.] I. Title. II. Series.
D1051.P48 1998
940—dc21   97–31009
                                                                                       CIP
                                                                                        AC

This picture, taken high above Earth, shows Europe, northern Africa, and western Asia. Europe is separated from Africa by the Mediterranean Sea. Europe and Asia are not separate land masses, but they are considered to be different continents.

Contents

Europe–The Cultural Continent   5

European Geography   10

The British Isles   19

Crowded Continent   24

The March of Progress   32

Into the Twenty-First Century   40

To Find Out More   44

Important Words   46

Index   47

Meet the Author   48

Europe— The Cultural Continent

If you ask your geography teacher about Europe, your teacher may say that Europe lies north of Africa, shares a border with Asia, and is the second-smallest of Earth's seven continents. And your teacher would be correct.

But is Europe really a separate continent? If you look at a map of the two continents, you'll notice that they make up one huge landmass. The only thing that divides them is a range of mountains in central Russia called the Ural Mountains.

No other continents are joined together like Europe and Asia. So why do we usually consider Europe and Asia to be separate?

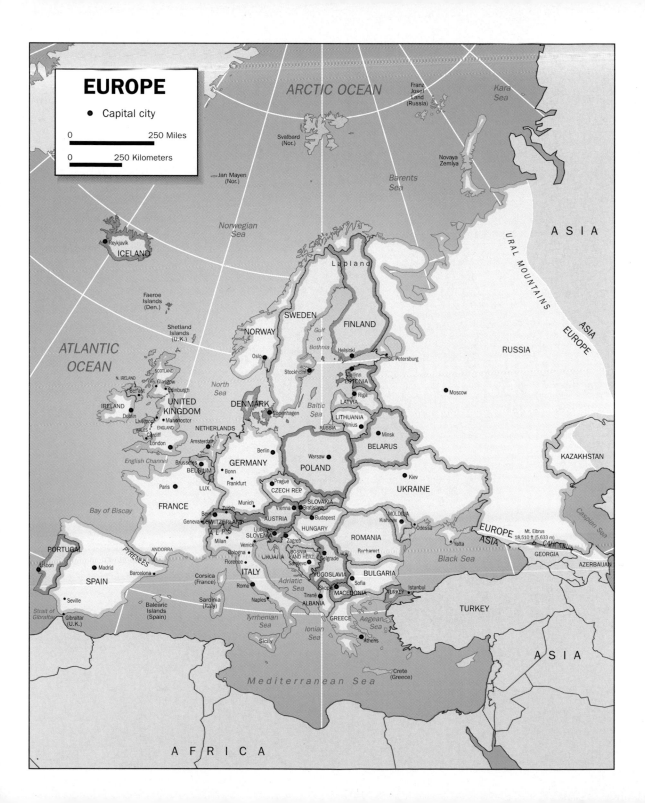

The low, rolling hills in the background are the Ural Mountains, which mark the border between Europe and Asia.

The answer has to do with culture. A culture is a large number of people who share the same race, language, religion, physical appearance, and homeland. People of the world belong to many cultures. When you cross the Ural Mountains, you will find different cultures on each side. This is why we think of Europe and Asia as separate continents.

These Russian people in St. Petersburg, located west of the Ural Mountains, are European. People from parts of Russia east of the Ural Mountains are Asian.

European Geography

The landscape of Europe is varied and lovely. Mountains rise up in many places—from low, rounded hills, to tall, snowcapped peaks.

The Pyrenees mountain range forms a border between Spain and France. The Alps run in a ragged line across France, Switzerland, Italy, and Austria.

The ski area pictured above is located in the Alps of Switzerland.

These majestic Alpine peaks are home to the world's most famous ski resorts.

But while the Alps are Europe's best-known mountains, they aren't the biggest. That title goes to the Caucasus Mountains. These mountains stand like a great stone wall between the Black and Caspian seas in southern Russia.

The highest peak in the Caucasus range is Mount Elbrus. At 18,510 feet (5,633 meters) above sea level, Elbrus is also Europe's highest point.

Europe's lowest point—the shore of the Caspian Sea—lies 92 feet (28 m) below sea level. Even though its water is salty,

A mountain climber (above) hikes Mount Elbrus, Europe's highest peak. A man rows a boat along the Volga River (right), Europe's longest river.

the Caspian Sea is surrounded by land, so it is actually the world's largest lake. Europe's longest river, the Volga, flows into the Caspian Sea from Russia in the northwest.

Most of Europe enjoys warm to mild summers and cool to cold winters. However, the northern regions of Finland, Sweden, Norway, and Russia—together called Lapland—are much colder. Lapland lies within the Arctic Circle, where the winters are long and bitterly cold. Lapland summers are short and cool.

The people who live in Lapland are sometimes called Lapps, but they refer to them-selves as Sami. Instead of

This family from the Norwegian part of Lapland poses in traditional Sami clothing with their reindeer (above). A team of huskies pulls a sled over the snow in the Swedish part of Lapland (right).

raising cattle and horses, Sami herd reindeer. Reindeer, which are part of the deer family, provide the Sami with food, transportation, clothing, and shelter. Their heavy, warm coats and big hooves allow them to survive arctic winters and walk over deep snow.

South of Lapland, the Great European Plain stretches across Russia, Poland, Belgium, Germany, France, and into southeastern England. This vast region of fertile, gently rolling land has some of the world's richest farmland.

The fertile fields of the Great European Plain cover much of Europe, including this region of France.

The Midnight Sun and the Northern Lights

This sequence of photographs shows the sun not quite setting during the Lapland summer.

The Northern Lights in Norway

In the middle of the summer, the sun never sets in Lapland. In the middle of the winter, however, the sun never rises. The Sami are used to these periods of twenty-four-hour daylight and twenty-four-hour darkness.

At times in the far north, a beautiful display of dazzling lights dances across the night sky. These Northern Lights are caused when particles from the sun hit Earth's atmosphere.

The British Isles

The British Isles are a group of islands off the coast of mainland Europe. These islands include Great Britain, Ireland, and some smaller islands nearby. Great Britain is separated from mainland Europe by the English Channel on the south and the

Waves crash against the shore of Land's End, the southwest tip of England (left). Cyclists ride past the rugged hills of Scotland (above).

North Sea on the east. Great Britain is made up of three countries—England, Scotland, and Wales. Ireland lies just to

This spectacular rock formation, called the Giant's Causeway, is located on the coast of Northern Ireland.

the west of Great Britain. Ireland is made up of two countries—the Republic of Ireland and Northern Ireland. Great Britain and Northern Ireland make up the United Kingdom.

The United Kingdom honors a royal family, though they do not govern the nation. Pictured here is Prince Charles (left), Queen Elizabeth II (center), and Prince Phillip (right).

Great Britain is only 20 miles (32 kilometers) from France. They are separated by a narrow stretch of water called the English Channel.

In the past, Great Britain has often been at war with countries in mainland Europe. Today, these countries are

Britain's friends and partners in trade. Helping to unite Great Britain with Europe is a brand-new transportation tunnel, sometimes called the Chunnel. Built beneath the English Channel, the Chunnel allows trains and cars to pass between England and France.

The Eurostar train carries passengers through the Chunnel between England and France.

Crowded Continent

Although Europe is the world's second-smallest continent, it has the world's second-largest human population. The reasons are clear. Europe has always been rich in things people need, including fertile farmland, fresh water, and a gentle climate.

This picture of Europe at night shows city lights as seen from space. The brighter areas are more heavily populated.

Also, travel is easy in Europe because there are few natural barriers, such as high mountain ranges or deserts, to get in the way. In fact, Europe is the only continent with no deserts at all.

Like many of the rivers in Europe, the Rhine River in Germany has provided easy boat transportation for centuries.

But Europe does have rivers, lots of rivers. These watery highways were especially important before the invention of trains, automobiles, and air-planes. Boats gliding along these rivers provided easy transportation throughout the continent.

Europe has a very long coastline with many natural harbors. These sheltered sea ports allow ships to come and go, safe from stormy seas.

Stockholm, Sweden, is one of the many European cities that grew up around a sheltered harbor.

For centuries, European nations controlled the seas. This sketch shows Christopher Columbus, an Italian explorer, sailing to America in 1492.

As a result, Europeans have ruled the seas for hundreds of years. Centuries ago, tall ships from England, Spain, France, Portugal, and Russia set sail. They went to explore, trade with, and conquer other nations around the globe.

These same European nations have long fought for control of their own continent. Europe has been divided into dozens of countries for hundreds of years. As the centuries passed, some European countries have disappeared and new nations have formed.

Today's Europe consists of forty-seven independent nations, including Russia, the world's largest country, and Vatican City, the world's smallest country. And the people of Europe speak about fifty different languages.

European nations have a long and bloody history. Two of the most destructive wars ever—World War I (1914–1918) and World War II (1939–1945)—began in Europe. Even today, fighting continues between different cultures in southeastern Europe.

Fortunately, most European governments have come to realize that they have more to

Peacekeeping forces from the United Nations take shelter as they come under attack in southeastern Europe in 1993.

gain by working together than by fighting. Across most of Europe, peace and cooperation have won the day.

The March of Progress

For most of Earth's history, there were no people in Europe. The first humans arrived there only about a million years ago. Traveling on foot from Africa, they crossed into Asia and then spread gradually north and west to populate Europe.

This stone monument, called Stonehenge, was built in southern England almost four thousand years ago. It is not clear exactly why it was built, but most experts think it had a religious purpose.

These early Europeans were nomads—they moved from place to place, hunting animals and gathering plants for food. They made tools and weapons of stone, bone, horn, and wood.

Until the late 1700s, most Europeans lived on farms.

Then, about eight thousand years ago, the people of Europe learned to farm. By growing crops and raising animals, large numbers of people could live in the same place year-round. The human population increased rapidly.

As their numbers grew, the people of Europe cut down huge forests. They needed more land for farming and more wood for building homes and making fires. The great forests of Europe began to disappear.

The next big change came to Europe in the late 1700s, with the Industrial Revolution. Large factories, powered by steam engines and other new inventions, sprang up in Europe's cities. Up to that time, most people lived in the countryside.

The Industrial Revolution brought many changes, some good and some bad. This illustration shows the trendous amount of pollution produced by the new factories.

They farmed the land or worked at home. But during the Industrial Revolution, more and more people moved to cities to look for jobs in the new factories.

Ever since the Industrial Revolution, most Europeans have lived in cities. This apartment building is in London, England.

Cities became larger and more crowded. Hundreds of miles of new railroads were built to provide easy travel between cities. Today, most Europeans live in or near cities.

A Land of

The Eiffel Tower in Paris was constructed in 1889 for the World's Fair.

Europe is home to many of the most historic buildings in the world. These are just a few of the continent's breath-taking structures.

Saint Peter's Church in Vatican City, Italy, is the world's largest Christian church. It was built during the 1500s and 1600s.

Landmarks

Westminster Abbey, the national church of England, was built in the 1200s.

The Palace of Versailles was built for the French king Louis XIV in the 1600s.

Into the Twenty-First Century

Most modern Europeans enjoy a high standard of living and great personal freedom. And because Europe was the birthplace of Western civilization, it has many splendid works of art and architecture, including the world's most

Europe is home to many breathtaking castles, such as this one in Bavaria, Germany.

magnificent castles, cathedrals, and museums.

Europe's big cities—such as London, Paris, Rome, Berlin, and Moscow—are bustling and exciting. Its small towns are charming, and farms and villages dot the countryside.

A street-side cafe (left) in Paris, France. These English schoolchildren (right) are some of the millions of friendly people who live in Europe.

Entering the twenty-first century, Europe is a safe and pleasant place to live. Its many attractions and rich culture draw millions of visitors each year. If you like history, art, music, great food, and friendly people, plan to visit Europe someday. By jet plane, it's only hours away!

Europe Fast Facts

Area 4,038,000 square miles (10,459,000 square kilometers)

Highest point Mount Elbrus, Russia: 18,510 feet (5,633 m) above sea level

Lowest point shore of the Caspian Sea, Russia: 92 feet (28 m) below sea level

Longest river Volga, Russia: 2,194 miles (3,531 km)

Largest lake Caspian Sea, Russia: 143,250 square miles (371,000 sq. km) in area

Number of independent nations 47

Population 713 million

To Find Out More

Here are some additional resources to help you learn more about the continent of Europe:

Books

Bullen, Susan. **The Alps and Their People.** Thomson Learning, 1994.

Burke, Patrick. **Eastern Europe.** Raintree Steck-Vaughn, 1997.

Dawson, Imogen. **Food and Feasts in the Middle Ages.** New Discovery Books, 1994.

Dunnan, Nancy. **One Europe.** Millbrook Press, 1992.

Gravett, Christopher. **Castle.** Alfred Knopf, 1994.

Hayes, Barbara and Robert Ingpen. **Folk Tales and Fables of Europe.** Chelsea House, 1994.

Macdonald, Fiona. **I Wonder Why Greeks Built Temples and Other Questions About Ancient Greece.** Kingfisher, 1997.

McHugh, Christopher. **Western Art: 1600–1800.** Thomson Learning, 1995.

McLeish, Ewan. **Europe.** Raintree Steck-Vaughn, 1997.

Steele, Philip. **Castles: Knights, Sieges, Jousts, Chivalry, Feasts.** Kingfisher, 1995.

Organizations and Online Sites

City Net—Europe
http://www.city.net/regions/europe/

This online guide offers information about many countries and cities in Europe.

Images of Europe
http://www.gorp.com/europeds/photogal/photogal.htm

This site features beautiful photographs of France and Switzerland.

INTELLiCast: Europe Weather
http://www.intellicast.com/weather/europe/

Forecasts and weather information for Europe.

The Irish Times
http://www.irish-times.com/

Learn about Ireland in this online newspaper.

The Louvre
http://mistral.culture.fr/louvre/louvrea.htm

This is the online site of the Louvre, a museum in Paris containing many of the world's most famous works of art.

Sweden Guide
http://www.swedenguide.com/

Offers information about all parts of Sweden.

Wandering Italy
http://www.wandering.com/

A guide to Italy including descriptions and photographs of Italy's major cities.

Important Words

architecture the designing of buildings

arctic regions of Earth lying close to the North Pole

colony a nation or area ruled by a foreign power

continent one of the seven large land masses of the earth

geography the study of Earth's continents, oceans, and other physical features

livestock farm animals, such as sheep and cattle

mainland the main landmass of a country or continent as opposed to its surrounding islands

majestic grand

nomad a person who moves from place to place in search of food

Index

(**Boldface** page numbers
  indicate illustrations.)

Agriculture, 16, **17,** 24,
  34, **34,** 41
Alps, the, 10, 11, **11**
Austria, 10
Belgium, 16
Berlin, Germany, 41
Black Sea, 12
British Isles, 19–23
Caspian Sea, 12–13, 13, 43
Caucasus mountains, 12
Culture, 8–9, 40–42
England, 16, 20, **20,** 23,
  28, **39**
English Channel, 19, 22,
  23
Finland, 14
France, 10, 16, **17,** 22,
  23, 28
Germany, 16, 26
Great Britain, 19, 20, 21,
  22–23
Industrial Revolution,
  35–36, **36**
Ireland, 19, 20–21
Italy, 10

Lapland, 14–16, **15,** 18,
  18
London, England, 41
Moscow, Russia, 41
Mount Elbrus, 12, **13,** 43
Northern Ireland, 21
Northern lights, 18, **18**
North Sea, 20
Norway, 14, **18**
Paris, France, **38,** 41, **42**
Poland, 16
Portugal, 28
Pyrenees, the, 10
Republic of Ireland, 21
Rhine River, 26
Rome, Italy, 41
Russia, 6, **9,** 12, 13, 14,
  16, 28, 29, 43
Sami, the, 14–16, **15,** 18
Scotland, 20, **20**
Spain, 10, 28
Stockholm, Sweden, 27
Sweden, 14, **15**
Switzerland, 10, **11**
Ural mountains, 6, **8,** 9
Vatican City, 29, **38**
Volga River, 13, 43
Wales, 20

Meet the Author

David Petersen lives in Colorado with his wife, Caroline, and two gigantic dogs, Otis and Angel. He enjoys reading, writing, hiking, camping, and dogs. His "grown-up" books include *Among the Elk* (Northland) and *A Hunter's Heart* (Henry Holt). Mr. Petersen has written many other books on geography for Children's Press, including True Books on all the continents.